DON'T GIVE UP, CHARLIE BROWN!

Artwork by
Charles M. Schulz

HARVEST HOUSE PUBLISHERS

EUGENE, OREGON

DON'T GIVE UP, CHARLIE BROWN!

ISBN-13: 978-0-7369-1524-3
ISBN-10: 0-7369-1524-9

TO

_____

FROM

_____

IF YOU GRIT YOUR TEETH,
YOU CAN'T FAIL!

CHARLIE BROWN

3

A stumble may prevent a fall.

THOMAS FULLER

ADVERSITY
BUILDS
CHARACTER...
WITHOUT
ADVERSITY A
PERSON COULD
NEVER MATURE
AND FACE UP
TO ALL OF THE
THINGS IN LIFE!

LUCY

When you get into a tight place and everything goes against you, till it seems as though you could not hang on a minute longer, never give up then, for that is just the place and time that the tide will turn.

HARRIET BEECHER STOWE

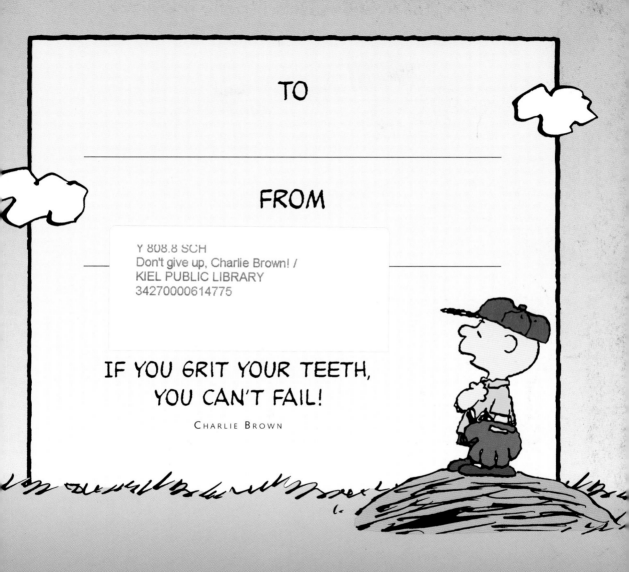

TO

_____

FROM

_____

IF YOU GRIT YOUR TEETH,
YOU CAN'T FAIL!

CHARLIE BROWN

3

A stumble may prevent a fall.

ADVERSITY
BUILDS
CHARACTER...
WITHOUT
ADVERSITY A
PERSON COULD
NEVER MATURE
AND FACE UP
TO ALL OF THE
THINGS IN LIFE!

LUCY

When you get into a tight place and everything goes against you, till it seems as though you could not hang on a minute longer, never give up then, for that is just the place and time that the tide will turn.

HARRIET BEECHER STOWE

4

To finish the moment, to find the journey's end in every step of the road, to live the greatest number of good hours, is wisdom.

Character cannot be developed
in ease and quiet. Only through
experience of trial and suffering
can the soul be strengthened,
vision cleared, ambition
inspired, and success achieved.

HELEN KELLER

6

Courage doesn't always roar. Sometimes courage is the quiet voice at the end of the day saying, "I will try again tomorrow."

LEARN FROM YESTERDAY...LIVE FOR TODAY...LOOK TO TOMORROW...REST THIS AFTERNOON.

SNOOPY

Far away there in the sunshine are my highest aspirations. I may not reach them, but I can look up and see their beauty, believe in them and try to follow where they lead.

LOUISA MAY ALCOTT

Anyone who doesn't make mistakes isn't trying hard enough.

WESS ROBERTS

If you think
you can,
you can.
And if you
think you can't,
you're right.

MARY KAY ASH

IT'S NOT HOW YOU START, IT'S HOW YOU FINISH.

PEPPERMINT PATTY

There is something good in all weathers. If it doesn't happen to be good for my work today, it's good for some other man's today, and will come around for me tomorrow.

CHARLES DICKENS

It is not raining rain to me,
It's raining daffodils;
In every dimpled drop I see
Wild flowers on the hills.

The clouds of gray engulf the day,
And overwhelm the town;
It is not raining rain to me,
It's raining roses down.

It is not raining rain to me,
But fields of clover bloom,
Where any buccaneering bee
May find a bed and room.

A health unto the happy!
A fig for him who frets;
It is not raining rain to me,
It's raining violets.

ROBERT LOVEMAN

THE RAIN FALLS ON THE JUST AND THE UNJUST.

CHARLIE BROWN

11

I think that if you shake the tree, you ought to be around when the fruit falls to pick it up.

MARY CASSATT

I do the very best I know how—the very best I can; and mean to keep doing so until the end.

ABRAHAM LINCOLN

IF YOU REALLY WANT SOMETHING IN THIS LIFE, YOU HAVE TO BE DETERMINED!

SPIKE

It is common sense to take a method and try it. If it fails, admit it frankly and try another. But above all, try something.

FRANKLIN D. ROOSEVELT

I'M SURE I'M GOING TO BE HAPPY, AND HAVE EVERYTHING GO JUST RIGHT FOR ME ALL THE DAYS OF MY LIFE!

LUCY

One of the things I learned the hard way was it does not pay to get discouraged. Keeping busy and making optimism a way of life can restore your faith in yourself.

LUCILLE BALL

I am not afraid
of tomorrow,
for I have seen
yesterday and
I love today.

WILLIAM ALLEN WHITE

15

Even if you're on
the right track
you'll get run over
if you just sit there.

WILL ROGERS

*Life is not meant to be easy,
my child; but take courage—
it can be delightful.*

GEORGE BERNARD SHAW

Only those who dare to fail greatly can ever achieve greatly.

ROBERT F. KENNEDY

LIFE IS FULL OF RISKS!

SNOOPY

I'VE ALWAYS BEEN FASCINATED BY FAILURE!

CHARLIE BROWN

Life's real failure is when you do not realize how close you were to success when you gave up.

AUTHOR UNKNOWN

The face of a friend, how it shines in the darkness
That often assails us; how preciously near
It seems, when the trial of long, long denial
Has made the sweetest blessings unspeakably dear!
The heart is consoled, and is lonely no longer,
Its terrors and tremors are all at an end,
And the way that was dreary becomes bright and cheery,
Illumined at once by the face of a friend.

AUTHOR UNKNOWN

19

The block of granite which was an obstacle
in the pathway of the weak becomes a
stepping-stone in the pathway of the strong.

THOMAS CARLYLE

*Keep on going and the chances are that you will stumble on
something, perhaps when you are least expecting it. I have
never heard of anyone stumbling on something sitting down.*

CHARLES F. KETTERING

You should treat all disasters as if they were trivialities, but never treat a triviality as if it were a disaster.

QUENTIN CRISP

A LITTLE TRAGEDY NOW AND THEN WILL MAKE YOU A BETTER PERSON!

LUCY

LIFE IS TOO SHORT NOT TO LIVE IT UP A LITTLE!

SNOOPY

The happiness of your life depends upon the quality of your thoughts; therefore guard accordingly.

MARCUS AURELIUS

Laffin' is the sensation of feelin' good all over but showin' it particularly in one spot.

JOSH BILLINGS

I THINK WE ALL FEAR THE UNKNOWN.

LINUS

Be not anxious about tomorrow. Do today's duty, fight today's temptations, and do not weaken nor distract yourself by looking forward to things which you cannot see, and could not understand if you saw them.

CHARLES KINGSLEY

It is God's wish that we grow in our faith.

MOTHER TERESA

I have found that most
people are about as
happy as they make up
their minds to be.

ABRAHAM LINCOLN

Trials, temptations,
disappointments—all
these are helps instead
of hindrances, if one
uses them rightly.
They not only test the
fiber of character, but
strengthen it…Every
trial endured and
weathered in the right
spirit makes a soul
nobler and stronger
than it was before.

JAMES BUCKHAM

I FEEL THE NEED TO HAVE THE FEELING THAT IT'S GOOD TO BE ALIVE.

SCHROEDER

The joy of spirit indicates its strength.

RALPH WALDO EMERSON

27

I've made it a practice to put all my worries down in the bottom of my heart, then set on the lid and smile.

MRS. WIGGS

TURN THE TV UP LOUD, CRAWL INTO
A BEANBAG WITH A BOWL OF ICE
CREAM AND DON'T THINK ABOUT IT.

SALLY

He is a wise man who does not grieve
for the thing which he has not, but
rejoices for those which he has.

EPICTETUS

Just whistle a bit, if your heart be sore
'Tis a wonderful balm for pain.
Just pipe some old melody o'er and o'er
Till it soothes like summer rain.

PAUL LAURENCE DUNBAR

IT'S NICE TO WAKE UP IN THE MORNING WITH A FEELING OF WELL-BEING.

SNOOPY

The habit of looking at the bright side of things is worth more than a thousand years.

SAMUEL JOHNSON

IF YOU GRIT YOUR TEETH, AND SHOW REAL

It is only by perseverance and tenaciousness that any object can be attained. "Impossible" is a word to be found only in the dictionary of fools.

NAPOLÉON BONAPARTE

We have no more need to be afraid of the step just ahead of us than we have to be afraid of the one just behind us.

FRANCES E. WILLARD

...ETERMINATION, YOU ALWAYS HAVE A CHANCE!

CHARLIE BROWN

Life is not so complex if we do not persist in making it so. We need faith; we need to be brave; we need chronically to keep the corners of the mouth turned up and not down. And after all it is only one step at a time.

RALPH WALDO EMERSON

33

We must
accept finite
disappointment,
but we must never
lose infinite hope.

MARTIN LUTHER KING

*The pleasantest
things in the
world are pleasant
thoughts, and the
great art in life is
to have as many of
them as possible.*

CHRISTIAN NESTELL BOVEE

EVERYONE NEEDS TO HAVE HOPE.

SNOOPY

Hope is a state of mind, not of the world. Hope, in
this deep and powerful sense, is not the same as joy
that things are going well, or willingness to invest in
enterprises that are obviously heading for success, but
rather an ability to work for something because it is good.

VACLAV HAVEL

YOU SHOULD START EACH DAY WITH
A SONG IN YOUR HEART, A GLEAM IN
YOUR EYE AND PEACE IN YOUR SOUL!

LUCY

If it were not for hopes, the heart would break.

Thomas Fuller

Life is either a daring
adventure or nothing.
To keep our faces
toward change and
behave like free spirits
in the presence of fate is
strength undefeatable.

Helen Keller

Hope is putting
faith to work
when doubting
would be easier.

AUTHOR UNKNOWN

Quite often we look at a task and think there is no way
we can do what needs to be done. That happens because
we look at ourselves when we should be looking at God.

JOYCE MEYER

IF YOU RELAX NOW AND THEN,
YOUR HEAD WON'T FALL OFF.

PEPPERMINT PATTY

WHENEVER I FEEL DEPRESSED, I BUILD SAND CASTLES.

LINUS

But we who feel the weight of the wheel when winter falls over our world can hope for tomorrow and raise our eyes to a silver moon in the open skies...

LESLIE FISH

What lies behind us and what lies before us are small matters compared to what lies within us.

RALPH WALDO EMERSON

41

Peace is a journey
of a thousand miles
and it must be taken
one step at a time.

LYNDON B. JOHNSON

Never fear shadows.
They simply mean
there's a light shining
somewhere nearby.

RUTH RENKEL

We are made strong by what we overcome.

JOHN BURROUGHS

ALL IT TAKES IS FAITH AND PATIENCE.

SPIKE

43

Prayer increases our ability to accept the present moment. You cannot live in the future, you cannot live in the past, you can only live in the now. The present moment is already exactly as it ought to be, even if we do not understand why it is as it is.

MATTHEW KELLY

It is possible to begin again. It is hard and we never do it perfectly, but it can be done…I must begin again on joy and happiness, on forgiveness and peace, on gratitude and patience.

ANDREW GREELEY

Hope and patience are two sovereign remedies for all, the surest reposals, the softest cushions to lean on in adversity.

ROBERT BURTON

WE ALL DO THINGS NOW AND THEN THAT
MAKE US LOSE CONFIDENCE IN OURSELVES.

CHARLIE BROWN

47

THE WORLD IS FILLED
WITH WONDERFUL THINGS.

Lucy

48